I0061275

GENDER EQUALITY AND SOCIAL INCLUSION DIAGNOSTIC FOR THE FINANCE SECTOR OF BANGLADESH

DECEMBER 2022

ASIAN DEVELOPMENT BANK

ADB

ISBN 978-92-9269-931-4 (print); 978-92-9269-932-1 (electronic); 978-92-9269-933-8 (ebook)
Publication Stock No. TCS220566-2
DOI: http://dx.doi.org/10.22617/TCS220566-2

Notes:
In this publication, "$" refers to United States dollars.
$1 = BDT84.50 as of June 2019.

Cover design by Jasper Lauzon.

CONTENTS

TABLES and FIGURE

FOREWORD

Gender equality in Bangladesh has improved with broad-based expansion. In the education sector, gender disparity has been eliminated in primary and secondary education and narrowed in tertiary education. Women's educational gains have led to better employment opportunities for women and increased the female labor force participation rate from 28.3% in 2000 to 36.3% in 2019. The economic contribution of women, particularly in the labor-intensive ready-made garment industry is substantial, which has helped change perceptions of women's economic and public roles. However, gender disparities remain an important social and economic issue in Bangladesh. There is a gender gap in financial literacy and numeracy, access to finance and financial services, and readiness to adopt digital finance. This not only affects women, but also has a multidimensional impact on women from disadvantaged and socially excluded groups such as transgender women, elderly and poor women, and women with disabilities.

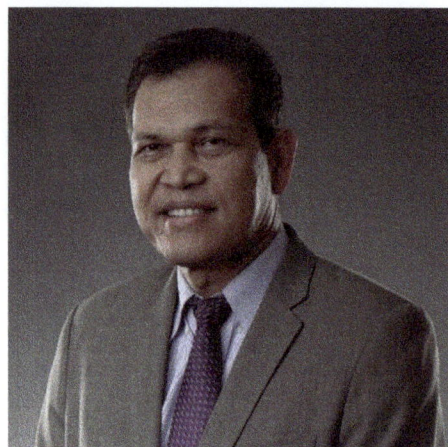

Exclusion is a multidimensional phenomenon that is not limited to material deprivation or specific sectors. Financial inclusion can provide pathways for all people, including the poor and disadvantaged, to expand their access to productive resources and, thus, contribute to inclusive development. Reducing gender inequality and all forms of exclusion in financial services can go a long way toward achieving sustainable and inclusive growth. Social inclusion is closely related to financial inclusion, so financial inclusion policies can contribute to social inclusion.

The priorities of the Asian Development Bank (ADB) for Bangladesh, as described in its Country Partnership Strategy: Bangladesh, 2021–2025, include improving the financial inclusion of the poor and excluded vulnerable groups, including women. Therefore, comprehensive action to mainstream gender equality and social inclusion (GESI) policies is essential to achieve ADB's goal of promoting social inclusion and development. ADB is committed to ensuring that all segments of society benefit from economic growth. ADB's priorities also include creating good jobs for all by improving the business environment for entrepreneurs and enterprises, including small and medium-sized enterprises (SMEs) and inclusive businesses, promoting the economic empowerment of women from diverse backgrounds, and addressing the non-income dimensions of poverty and vulnerability.

These actions are in line with Bangladesh's national policies and strategies, including the Bangladesh National Strategy for Social Security and the Eighth Five-Year Plan, which have adopted gender equality and inclusion strategies for "ethnic minorities, physically challenged and underprivileged groups" as a core part of poverty reduction and inclusive growth.

This report highlights the gaps from a GESI perspective to understand how financial services can be inclusive and provide access to financial and productive resources to leave no one behind. Particular attention is given to addressing GESI in SME finance, as SMEs play a critical role in inclusive development.

We hope that the recommendations and key findings of the report will provide concrete guidance to both ADB and the government in identifying entry points for greater visibility and effectiveness of GESI aspects in the design and implementation of ADB-financed projects by drawing on lessons learned from ongoing and past initiatives.

Edimon Ginting
Country Director
Bangladesh Resident Mission
Asian Development Bank

MESSAGE

Financial inclusion has been a key focus of the Government of
Bangladesh, especially in terms of ensuring that every individual
and business has equitable and easy access to financial services and
products. This commitment has been appropriately reflected in various
national strategy documents including the Eighth Five-Year Plan (8FYP),
National Strategy for Social Security, the National Women Development
Policy 2011, National Financial Inclusion Strategy (2021–2025),
and others. Focusing on different entry points, the strategic objective
of all these policy documents has been to enhance women's access
to and control over productive resources through better access to
financial services.

Bangladesh's finance sector has embraced technology solutions paired with rapid financial growth to
improve the financial inclusion of the general population. Apart from women, financially excluded groups
comprise socially disadvantaged groups such as transgender and small ethnic minorities, small and marginal
farmers, persons with disabilities, self-employed and unorganized sector employees, urban slum dwellers,
migrants, and older people.

Given the importance of financial inclusion for sustainable economic development in leveraging ways to
expand people's access to productive resources and, thus, contributing to the country's overall inclusive
development, reducing gender inequality and all forms of exclusion in financial services is imperative to
achieving sustainable and inclusive growth in the country.

This report aims to understand the gaps in achieving gender equality and social inclusion (GESI) in financial
services in Bangladesh. It gives a special attention to addressing GESI in small and medium-sized enterprise
(SME) financing, as SMEs play a vital role in inclusive development.

Another focus of the report is the role of digital/mobile financial services (DFS/MFS) in enhancing financial
inclusion. This is a response to the need to highlight promising innovations in this sector, and the fact
that 8FYP aims to make the DFS/MFS system more effective in achieving financial inclusion of poor and
disadvantaged groups.

This report will contribute greatly to the dialogue among government and key stakeholders in identifying
the examples and lessons presented here to focus narrowly on financial services and products, and on
interventions related to different aspects of the sector including solutions for inclusive access to financial
services and products.

The attention given to women, and especially women SME entrepreneurs, in finance policies, programs, and institutional arrangements will help shape future policies and programs undertaken by the government for greater financial inclusion in the country.

Fatima Yasmin
Senior Secretary
Finance Division, Ministry of Finance
Government of the People's Republic of Bangladesh

ABBREVIATIONS

8FYP	Eighth Five-Year Plan
ADB	Asian Development Bank
ADBI	Asian Development Bank Institute
BB	Bangladesh Bank
BDT	Bangladesh taka
BWCCI	Bangladesh Women Chamber of Commerce and Industry
CMSMEs	cottage, micro, small, and medium-sized enterprises
CPS	Country Partnership Strategy
DFI	development finance institution
DFS	digital financial services
FCB	foreign commercial bank
FII	Financial Inclusion Insights
FY	fiscal year
GAP	gender action plan
GDP	gross domestic product
GESI	gender equality and social inclusion
GSMA	Global System for Mobile Communications
ID	identification
IFC	International Finance Corporation
KYC	know-your-customer
MFI	microfinance institution
MFS	mobile financial services
MSMEs	micro, small, and medium-sized enterprises
NBFI	nonbank financial institution
NFIS-B	National Financial Inclusion Strategy–Bangladesh
NSSS	National Strategy for Social Security
NWDP	National Women Development Policy
OP	Operational Priority
PCB	private commercial bank
PKSF	*Palli Karma Sahayak Foundation*
PO	partner organization
PWDs	persons with disabilities
RMG	ready-made garments
SB	scheduled bank
SCB	state-owned commercial bank
SIM	subscriber identity module
SMEF	SME Foundation
SMEs	small and medium-sized enterprises
SMESPD	SME and Special Programs Department
TA	technical assistance

EXECUTIVE SUMMARY

Over the years, Bangladesh has made impressive progress on eradicating poverty and enhancing human development. Yet various forms of exclusion, particularly exclusion associated with gender, persist. Meanwhile, social inclusion is closely correlated with financial inclusion. As such, comprehensive action on mainstreaming gender equality and social inclusion (GESI) is essential to achieve the aim of the Asian Development Bank (ADB) in promoting social inclusion and development. The present report aims to understand the gaps that exist with regard to achieving GESI in financial services in Bangladesh.

Financial inclusion refers to the provision of access to financial services to all people in a fair, transparent, and equitable manner at an affordable cost. Bangladesh's finance sector[1] has undergone rapid growth and has embraced technology solutions to improve the population's financial inclusion. However, there are still gender gaps and exclusion in financial literacy, financial numeracy, access to finance and financial services, and readiness to adopt digital financing, all of which prevent women from benefiting from existing financial services.

Several national planning documents, policies, and regulations cover financial inclusion as a tool for development. These include the Eighth Five-Year Plan 2020–2025, the National Strategy for Social Security 2015, the National Women Development Policy 2011, the National Financial Inclusion Strategy 2021–2025, and others. Albeit with a focus on different entry points, the strategic objective of all these policy documents is to enhance women's access to and control over productive resources through better access to financial services.

Key female financial inclusion issues and gaps in Bangladesh include those related to access (about 65% of women are unbanked); the gender gap in mobile phone ownership, necessary for mobile financial services, is about 30%); loan disbursement (only 7% of small and medium-sized borrowers are women); demand-side obstacles (e.g., unfamiliarity with bank procedures); supply-side challenges (e.g., location of bank branches, social norms, and others); lack of credible sex-disaggregated data; and low female participation in the sector workforce (only 15% of the workforce is female and women occupy only around 8% of the top-level positions).

Several initiatives, by different organizations, have aimed to ensure financial inclusion for women, through various financial solutions. Women-focused products offered by different banks include bank account services with higher deposit rates for women, debit and credit card facilities with special privileges, low-cost loan facilities for women entrepreneurs, business support advisory services, and consumer loans at preferential interest rates. Some examples are City Bank's *City Alo*, Green Delta Insurance's *Nibedita Comprehensive Insurance Policy for Women*, and a partnership between bKash and Shakti Foundation providing credit to women directly.

---

[1]   The sector includes various types of banks, the insurance sector, microfinance institutions, mobile financial services, and others.

ADB's country partnership strategy for Bangladesh (2021–2025) commits to expanding integrated support for women entrepreneurs and women-led small and medium-sized enterprises through better access to finance, adoption of new technologies, and policy and institutional reforms. The seven finance sector-related projects of ADB focus on gender mainstreaming. In looking ahead, ADB might concentrate on a few issues, among others, to enhance the financial inclusion of women in the context of GESI: supporting microenterprises owned by women, employing more women as finance sector workers, developing special insurance products and services for women, more digital and mobile inclusion for women, and the generation more sex-disaggregated data.

1 Introduction

In Bangladesh, significant progress has been made in terms of reducing poverty and providing equal access to quality health and education for all. Despite these achievements, inequality and various forms of exclusion, associated with gender, age (older people, youth, and children), disability, social identity, sexual and gender identity, geographic location, and income status[1] persist in the country.

Exclusion is a multidimensional phenomenon, not limited to material deprivation or specific sectors. As such, comprehensive action to mainstream gender equality and social inclusion (GESI) is essential to achieve the aim of the Asian Development Bank (ADB) in promoting social inclusion and development. ADB is committed to ensuring all members of society benefit from growth. Its priorities include generating good jobs for all by improving the business environment for entrepreneurs and companies, including small and medium-sized enterprises (SMEs) and inclusive businesses; promoting economic empowerment of women of different backgrounds; and addressing the non-income dimensions of poverty and vulnerability in urban and rural areas.[2] In other words, ADB intends to provide technical assistance to its South Asia developing members to enhance GESI.[3] This is aligned with the national policy documents of Bangladesh, including the National Strategy for Social Security (NSSS) 2015[4] and the Eighth Five-Year Plan (8FYP) 2020–2025, which have adopted gender equality and inclusion strategies for *"ethnic minorities, physically challenged and under-privileged groups"* as core to poverty reduction and inclusive growth.[5]

Social inclusion is closely correlated with financial inclusion, and policies for financial inclusion can contribute to social inclusion.[6] Specifically for Bangladesh, ADB's current priorities include "enhancing financial inclusion for the poor and excluded vulnerable groups, including women" (footnote 1, p. 10). Together with enhanced access to basic services, this will contribute to ADB's strategic objective for Bangladesh to "strengthen human capital and social protection" (footnote 1, p. 15).

Financial inclusion refers to the provision of access to financial services to all people in a fair, transparent, and equitable manner at an affordable cost.[7] It is a powerful determinant of sustainable economic development.

---

[1] ADB. 2021. *Country Partnership Strategy: Bangladesh, 2021–2025—Sustain Growth, Build Resilience, and Foster Inclusion*. Manila.

[2] Two key operational priorities of ADB, mentioned in its Strategy 2030, are addressing remaining poverty and reducing inequalities (priority 1) and accelerating progress in gender equality (priority 2) (ADB. 2018. *Strategy 2030: Achieving a Prosperous, Inclusive, Resilient, and Sustainable Asia and the Pacific*. Manila).

[3] ADB. 2020. *Enhancing Gender Equality and Social Inclusion Results in South Asia Developing Member Countries*. Manila.

[4] General Economics Division, Bangladesh Planning Commission, Government of Bangladesh. 2020. *Midterm Progress Review on Implementation of the National Social Security Strategy*. Dhaka.

[5] General Economics Division, Bangladesh Planning Commission, Government of Bangladesh. 2020. *Eighth Five-Year Plan (July 2020–June 2025), Promoting Prosperity and Fostering Inclusiveness*. Dhaka. p. xlix.

[6] P. Ozili. 2020. Social Inclusion and Financial Inclusion: International Evidence. *Munich Personal RePEc Archive Paper*. No. 101811.

[7] Bangladesh Bank. 2019. *Survey on Impact Analysis of Access to Finance in Bangladesh*. Dhaka.

It leverages ways to expand people's access to productive resources, thus, contributing to the country's overall inclusive development. Reducing gender inequality and all forms of exclusion in financial services can go a long way toward achieving such sustainable and inclusive growth. Financial inclusion can improve access to finance for all members of society by providing microcredit as a social policy to reduce poverty, liberalizing credit to households, and promoting financial innovation such as digital finance to all individuals (footnote 6).

Bangladesh's finance sector has embraced technology solutions paired with rapid financial growth to improve the financial inclusion of the general population. However, widespread gender gaps and exclusion remain in different aspects of financial services. Apart from women, financially excluded sections of the population comprise groups such as small and marginal farmers, tenant farmers, landless laborers, self-employed and unorganized sector employees, urban slum dwellers, migrants, ethnic minorities, and poor senior citizens (footnote 7).

There is a gender gap in financial literacy and numeracy, access to finance and financial services, and readiness to adopt digital financing, as mentioned above. What affects women in this field is not only their gender. Rather, gender often combines with other factors—for example, disability or older age, being a member of a poorer segment in society, being from an ethnic minority or a remote geographical location—leading to extreme forms of financial and social exclusion. The gender policy of the NSSS recognizes this disparity and aims to empower women so they can achieve control over productive resources through government to private sector cash transfers, affordable financial services (microcredit, education loans, saving accounts), and the simplification of other banking services (footnote 4). Persons with disabilities (PWDs) have no access to leading lending sources in Bangladesh because of discrimination and accessibility barriers, including negative attitudes, lack of economic opportunities, and the unpaid or underpaid nature of work.[8] Many economically active PWDs do not have access to affordable financial products and services.[9] It should be stressed at this stage that detailed information on the financial inclusion of other disadvantaged groups, such as *hijras,* is scarce, and this represents an additional obstacle to progress in their social inclusion.

The above paragraphs provide the rationale for this report, as they highlight ADB's concern for both gender equality and social inclusion, and the role that financial inclusion can play in enhancing women's economic empowerment and productivity, and those of disadvantaged groups, as well as in contributing to the broader aim of sustainable development. As already mentioned, when referring to women, the report stresses that their exclusion and vulnerability are not a result merely of their gender, and highlights how other elements, for example, education, age, class, or ethnic origin, contribute. Thus, it takes an intersectional approach.

---

[8]   J. Smolen. 2014. *Financial Inclusion of Disabled People in Bangladesh: The Broken Promises of MFIs.*

[9]   D. Sarker. 2020. *How Do Economically Active People with Disabilities Access Microfinance?* Paper prepared for Australasian Aid Conference 2020. Canberra. 17–19 February.

This report aims to understand the gaps in achieving GESI in financial services in Bangladesh. It gives special attention to addressing GESI in SME financing, as SMEs play a vital role in inclusive development. This focus reflects the sheer scale of the SME sector in the country, which accounts for an estimated 25% of Bangladesh's gross domestic product (GDP).[10] In addition, many SMEs and microenterprises are part of the informal sector,[11] where a larger share of those employed are female (91.8% versus 82.1% male). Conditions in the informal sector are characterized by absence of formal contracts, low security of employment and limited earnings, absence of social security programs and trade union support, and limited financial inclusion opportunities.

Another focus of the report is the role of digital/mobile financial services (DFS/MFS) in enhancing financial inclusion. This is a response to the need to highlight promising innovations in this sector, and the fact that 8FYP aims to make the DFS/MFS system more effective in achieving financial inclusion of poor and disadvantaged groups (footnote 5).

Finally, the analysis attempts to identify entry points for greater visibility and effectiveness of GESI aspects in the design and implementation of ADB-financed projects, by relying on lessons learned during ongoing and past initiatives. The report is based on an analysis of secondary data and information.

---

[10] S. A. Sultana. 2021. *Women Entrepreneurs in Bangladesh: Barely Staying Afloat.*

[11] S. Raihan. 2010. Informal Sector in Bangladesh: Implications for Growth and Poverty. *Indian Journal of Labour Economics.* 53(2). pp. 251–265.

2 Context of the Finance Sector in Bangladesh

The finance sector of Bangladesh includes banks and nonbank financial institutions (NBFIs), capital market intermediaries, insurance companies, and microfinance institutions (MFIs). Banks include state-owned commercial banks (SCBs), private commercial banks (PCBs), foreign commercial banks (FCBs), and development finance institutions (DFIs). There is also a reasonably large informal finance sector comprising unregulated lenders, including individuals or informal cooperatives. The expansion of financial institutions and the increased availability of various financial products and initiatives to reduce the rural–urban gap in financial services in recent years have encouraged the financial inclusion of women and disadvantaged groups. These are discussed in subsequent sections; this section provides an overview of the formal finance sector of Bangladesh in relation to GESI.

Banks

Immediately after Bangladesh obtained independence in 1971, the banking sector started up, with six nationalized commercialized banks, three state-owned specialized banks, and nine foreign banks. The sector expanded gradually with the entry of private banks in the 1980s. During the 1990s, more private banks entered the sector. There are now (as of 2019) 59 scheduled banks and 5 nonscheduled banks in Bangladesh.[12] The scheduled banks include SCBs, PCBs, specialized banks (for agricultural or industrial development), and FCBs. There was rapid growth (by over 53.6%) in bank branches between 2008 and 2019, mainly because of notable growth (close to 152%) in branch expansion by PCBs. PCBs as a group have become even more dominant in the banking market, although 64% of their branches are situated in urban areas.

SCBs play an essential role in extending banking facilities to rural areas, as they have an urban–rural branch ratio of 37:63. In the case of the DFIs, almost all branches (92%) are in rural areas. No foreign bank has branches in rural areas.

A circular letter issued in 2006 by Bangladesh Bank (BB) asked that banks set up one rural branch for every four branches in urban areas to increase financial inclusion for rural people.[13] This was an important initiative for enhancing social inclusion in financial services, as rural people tend to have less access to financial institutions. In 2012, opening bank branches became more pro-rural, as BB asked for one rural

---

[12] **Scheduled banks** in Bangladesh are those operating under the full control and supervision of Bangladesh Bank (BB) (the central bank), which is empowered to do so through BB Order 1972 and the Bank Company Act 1991. **Nonscheduled banks** are established for a special and definite objective and cannot perform all the functions of scheduled banks (Bangladesh Bank. Banks and FIs).

[13] Bangladesh Bank. 2006. *BRPD Circular Letter No. 2*. Dhaka.

branch for every urban branch.[14] These banking regulations may have profoundly influenced the placement of branches in rural areas. However, the number of rural branches is still low, which may be because of the small size of rural subdistricts.[15] All the same, this regulation resulted in a substantial increase in rural branches, mainly in PCBs (column 5 of Table 1). While in 2008, 28% of total branches of PCBs were situated in rural areas, the share of rural branches had risen to 36% in 2019. The number of branches of PCBs also increased during this period, from 2,082 to 5,257. Though the percentage of rural units declined in the case of SCBs, this has not meant a decline in financial inclusion in rural areas, as the proportion of rural branches was very high for SCBs in 2008 (63%) and more urban branches in later periods brought a balance between urban and rural areas, as mentioned earlier.

PCBs constitute the highest share of total assets in banks (67.8%, 2019) and total deposits in all banks (68.1%). Both shares have increased since 2008. An increase in assets and deposits and the rise in the number of rural branches in PCBs indicate that more rural people use such banking services. However, while expanding bank branches in rural areas may indicate increased social inclusion of financial services in these localities, there is limited data on how various disadvantaged groups, including older people, PWDs, and transgender people use the services made available by this expansion.

Table 1: Comparing the Broad Structure of the Banking Sector, 2008 and 2019

Bank Type	Year	Number of Bank Type	Total Number of Branches	Urban–Rural Branch Ratio[a]	Total Assets of Bank (BDT billion)	Share of Bank Type in Total Assets (%)	Total Deposits in Bank (BDT billion)	Share of Bank Type in Total Deposits (%)
1	2	3	4	5	6	7	8	9
SCB	2008	4	3,386	37:63	1,030.9	31.11	758.8	29.62
	2019	6	3,773	47:53	3,995.4	24.51	3,038.6	25
PCB	2008	30	2,082	72:28	1,794.5	54.16	1,450.7	56.64
	2019	41	5,257	64:36	11,048.2	67.8	8,269.6	68.1
FCB	2008	9	56	100:0	265.8	8.02	214.1	8.36
	2019	9	65	100:0	897.2	5.5	524.4	4.3
SB	2008	5	1,359	11:89	222.3	6.71	137.8	5.38
	2019	3	11,483	19:81	357.5	2.2	312.7	2.6
Total	2008	48	6,886	42:58	3,313.5	100	2,561.4	100
	2019	59	10,578	51:49	16,298.4	100	12,145.2	100

BDT = Bangladesh taka, FCB = foreign commercial bank, PCB = private commercial bank, SB = scheduled bank, SCB = state-owned commercial bank.

a Urban–rural branch ratio refers to the percentage of bank branches situated in rural and urban areas for a particular type of bank.

Sources: Bangladesh Bank Annual Reports 2008–09 and 2019–20.

---

14   Bangladesh Bank. 2012. *BRPD Circular Letter No. 18*. Dhaka.

15   K. Iqbal, P. K. Roy, and S. Alam. 2018. Regional Variations of Banking Services and Poverty Reduction: Evidence from Subdistrict Level Administrative Data of Bangladesh. *Working Paper Series*. No. 871. Tokyo: Asian Development Bank Institute.

Nonbank Financial Institutions

The number of NBFIs was 34 as of June 2019, having increased from 29 in 2008, with 273 branches spread all over the country (in both rural and urban areas) (Table 2). Although the growth rates of deposits and advances of NBFIs were higher than those of banks during the 2008–2019 period, NBFIs remained an insignificant part of financial institutions.

NBFIs play an active role in financial inclusion by expanding various deposit and credit facilities, both at the individual level and to industries, especially SMEs. In addition, some of these NBFIs have special credit facilities for women entrepreneurs, which have a concessional rate and easy terms.[16]

Table 2: Comparing the Broad Structure of the Nonbank Financial Institution Sector, 2008 and 2019

	2008	2019
NBFI Type		
Government	1	3
Joint venture	8	13
Private	20	19
Total NBFIs	**29**	**34**
Total branches	80	273
Total assets (BDT billion)	142.4	871.5
Total deposits (BDT billion)	38.3	451.9

BDT = Bangladesh taka, NBFI = nonbank financial institution.
Sources: Bangladesh Bank Annual Reports 2012–13 and 2019–20.

Microfinance Institutions

Although the volume of advances and deposits of MFIs has not been very significant during the past 10 years as compared with those of the banking industry, their benefits have reached a sizable number of low-income rural people, especially women. In fiscal year (FY) 2019/20,[17] the 759 licensed MFIs disbursed more than Bangladesh taka (BDT) 1,352 billion to more than 30 million borrowers, and the total savings of the microfinance sector was more than BDT302.0 billion.[18] Together with banks, MFIs have contributed to higher intensity of financial deepening, and access to financial services is rising continuously in Bangladesh.[19]

---

[16]   One such example is a credit facility for women entrepreneurs termed *Joyee* offered by IPDC Finance Limited (IPDC SME Financing).
[17]   In Bangladesh, the fiscal year runs from July to June.
[18]   Bangladesh Bank. 2020. *Annual Report 2019–20*. Dhaka.
[19]   M. A. B. Khalily. 2016. Financial Inclusion, Financial Regulation, and Education in Bangladesh. *Working Paper Series*. No. 621. Tokyo: Asian Development Bank Institute.

Palli Karma Sahayak Foundation (PKSF) works as an apex microcredit funding and training organization for alleviating poverty by providing microcredit to the poor through its partner organizations (POs).[20] It disbursed loans to 278 POs of BDT38.7 billion in FY2019/20, BDT1.7 billion or 4.5% higher than the BDT37.0 billion in FY2018/19. PKSF works to empower women in terms of human capability as well as economic and social opportunities.[21] The POs supervise and monitor their women beneficiaries as they learn to manage financial and nonfinancial services they access from the POs. Access to financial services offered by PKSF (through its POs) is tied to various other programs that are intended for women's empowerment and social inclusion. In addition, these initiatives include training programs, social awareness programs, and special services for disabled people and other disadvantaged groups. For example, PKSF implemented a project titled *Ujjibito* under which it included disability-friendly mobile training facilities and livelihood activities suitable for transgender people.[22]

Other large MFIs, like Grameen Bank, BRAC, and ASA, have also added different programs for women's empowerment and for social inclusion to their microfinance operations. These activities are enhancing financial inclusion and the social status of the poor. Moreover, microcredit, skills development training, technical assistance, primary healthcare services, and awareness-building campaigns make the labor market work better, remove gender inequalities, and increase financial inclusion.[23] Although microfinance has been used widely in Bangladesh as a tool for reducing poverty and empowering poor people, still few MFIs are providing microfinance to PWDs (footnote 9).

Agent Banking

Agent banking as an emerging financial inclusion tool provides access to tailormade financial products to segments of the underserved population, including women. Agent banking uses agents as intermediaries to extend banking services, rather than the common practice of having branches as intermediaries. An agent or a person from a locality agrees with a commercial bank to open a banking outlet to offer essential banking services of savings and lending. In this way, banks can extend their services to rural areas cost-effectively without setting up a branch or employing their officials. Banking services can be developed significantly through agent banks in geographically remote locations where branch establishment is extremely difficult or not feasible.[24]

---

[20]   PKSF provides assistance through different nongovernment, semi-government, and government organizations; voluntary agencies and societies; local government bodies; institutions; groups; and individuals. These organizations and institutions are largely called partner organizations (POs). PKSF receives funds from the government, which are lent to POs at a certain rate of interest to conduct their (mostly microcredit) operations. PKSF operates with interest earning and yearly funds from the government. Together with different financial support such as microcredit, micro savings, and microinsurance, PKSF assists its POs in their institutional development, monitors their activities, and suggests initiation of effective livelihood activities.

[21]   Q. K. Ahmed. 2017. *Time to Champion Women's Empowerment: Implementation of SDGs in Bangladesh.*

[22]   Ujjibito. *Food Security 2012 Bangladesh Ujjibito.*

[23]   N. Akhter. 2018. Women Empowerment and Microfinance: A Case from North-Western Bangladesh. *Asian Development Perspective.* 9(1). pp. 35–50.

[24]   Establishing a bank branch requires both a suitable physical setup and human resources. It may be difficult to establish branches in areas that are remote in terms of communications (road and/or railways), less attractive in terms of arranging accommodations for bank officials, prone to natural calamities, and others. In such areas, agent banking through a local person (the agent) and simple physical infrastructure may serve the purpose of providing basic banking services.

Given that, in certain geographical locations, distance constrains people, especially women, from using banking services, agent banking can enhance gender equality in financial services (footnote 7). An intersectional approach helps us see that agent banking is particularly important for rural women, given their relatively limited mobility and access to information (compared with that for males). Moreover, women from households that rely on remittances have found agent banks to be an accessible medium for use in receiving these. This may also be true for disadvantaged groups such as PWDs and transgender people—whoever is constrained by distance and time. However, we do not have data on the extent to which these groups use this service.

Although BB issued an agent banking guideline in 2013, full-fledged agent operations started only in 2016.[25] As of September 2020, 28 banks had been licensed for agent banking, and 24 were actively engaged.[26] A total of 10,163 agents had been engaged with 14.016 outlets,[27] which was, respectively, 55.61% and 49.25% more than in the previous fiscal year. Out of all the agent banking outlets, 87% were situated in rural areas. The promotion of agent banking services to the rural population had led to growth in financial inclusion overall and among the rural poor. The total number of accounts up to September 2020 was 8.2 million, of which 45.6% were accounts owned by women, up from 34.6% in 2018 (of 5.3 million accounts in total in that year). These numbers point to considerable adoption of agent banking among women (see figure). However, we do not have sex-disaggregated data on the gender balance among service providers or agents.

Account Holders in Agent Banking and Share of Female Account Holders, 2018–2020

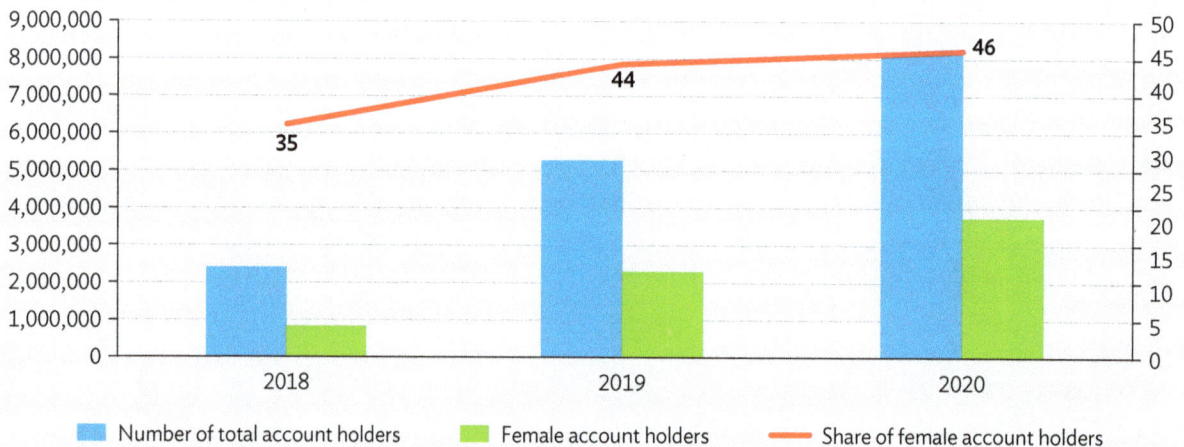

Source: M. S. Ahsan et al. 2013. The Microinsurance Market in Bangladesh: An Analytical Overview. *Bangladesh Development Studies*. 36(1). pp. 1–54.

---

[25]   S. Islam. 2018. The Rapid Growth of Agent Banking in Bangladesh. *Dhaka Times*. 3 June.

[26]   The other four banks have the license, but have not started agent banking activities.

[27]   A small office of the agent serving the banking operations.

Mobile Financial Services

The rapid countrywide expansion of mobile phone networks and the exponential growth in subscribers have opened up opportunities for introducing innovative mobile phone-based off-branch financial services. Utilizing this opportunity, MFS have been experiencing remarkable growth since their inception in 2011. Initially, MFS was only a payment instrument; later, it became a medium of deposit mobilization also. BB has introduced a tiered know-your-customer (KYC) and electronic documentation system for opening an MFS account, further accelerating financial inclusion. In the early stages, MFS transactions were limited to cash-in/cash-out. In contrast, later, BB allowed many other modes of transactions, including person-to-person, person-to-business, business-to-person, person-to-government, and government-to-person. In this way, MFS have become one of the key drivers of financial inclusion through providing services to population segments otherwise excluded (those who do not have bank accounts, people with limited mobility, those living in remote areas, and others).

According to BB, since the inception of MFS, the flow of money into the rural parts of Bangladesh has been increasing significantly. As of June 2019, 15 banks and 1 subsidiary of the bank had been permitted to provide MFS (footnote 18). The number of registered and active mobile bank accounts stood at $852,941.2 and $382,352.9, respectively. An impact study of MFS, initiated by BB, found that MFS were helping people living in rural areas to transfer money easily and purchase online content. MFS also help families when they suffer from shortages of money, groceries, medicines, fertilizers, and others.[28] MFS are, thus, having significant impacts on the family life of Bangladeshi people.

Insurance Sector

The insurance sector has immense potential to accelerate access to finance in Bangladesh. In 2011, the Insurance Development and Regulatory Authority was instituted as the regulator of the industry, with a mandate to protect the interests of policyholders and other stakeholders under the insurance policy, to supervise and regulate the industry effectively, and to ensure orderly and systematic growth of the industry. The insurance industry comprises 78 (32 life and 46 general) operating companies. Insurance services include life insurance, general insurance, reinsurance, microinsurance, and *takaful*, or Islamic, insurance. A BB survey found that, at the end of 2017, the number of depositors was 15,854,037, of whom life insurance depositors numbered 14,384,763 and nonlife insurance depositors 1,469,274. In the same period, the number of deposit accounts was 16,929,191, of which life insurance deposit accounts were 14,618,867 and nonlife insurance deposit accounts 2,310,324 (footnote 7). The survey also found that, out of 2,872 respondents (38% female), only 14% had various types of insurance policies, and 42% did not have any idea about insurance policies. The adoption rate was higher for the banked respondents (17%) than for the unbanked respondents (8%). This implies that disadvantaged people who do not have a bank account also possibly do not have an insurance policy of any kind. The survey does not offer information on other excluded or vulnerable groups. Therefore, there is a gap in the knowledge on the behavior of such groups with regard to adopting and accessing insurance policies.

---

[28]   Bangladesh Bank. 2017. *An Impact Study on Mobile Financial Services (MFSs) in Bangladesh.* Joint study by the Bangladesh Bank and University of Dhaka.

The insurance products mentioned above target mainly high- and medium-income people. Microinsurance products provided by MFIs cover various types of insurance support to low-income people. Microinsurance services are affordable risk-shifting devices offered by insurers that are especially suited to the needs of such low-income households. They offer loan insurance to minimize lenders' risks and to enable a quicker claim settlement process.[29] In addition, microinsurance products include various health insurance schemes, livestock insurance, and microenterprise insurance. As most of the beneficiaries in MFIs are women, microinsurance provided by the MFIs, in turn, helps women mitigate various life and economic risks. However, most of these microinsurance schemes are not examples of true insurance products, since the bulk of the risk eventually remains with the insured (footnote 29). There is also a Deposit Insurance System in the banking sector, which protects bank depositors, especially tiny depositors, from losses caused by a bank's inability to pay its debts when due.

Capital Market

The capital market is considered the second-largest segment of the financial system in Bangladesh. It provides funds for long-term investment and development and, in this way, contributes to economic growth. The capital market comprises Dhaka Stock Exchange and Chittagong Stock Exchange. The instruments in these exchanges are equity securities (shares), debentures, and corporate bonds. We do not have data on the participation of women in capital market operations.

---

[29]   M. S. Ahsan et al. 2013. The Microinsurance Market in Bangladesh: An Analytical Overview. *Bangladesh Development Studies*. 36(1). pp. 1–54.

3 Policy Context for Addressing Gender Inequality and Social Inclusion in the Finance Sector

Key Regulatory Institutions for the Finance Sector

BB, the central bank of Bangladesh, guides and controls the financing operations and activities of banks and NBFIs mainly associated with non-securities financial instruments and markets. Functions and activities linked to securities instruments by banks and NBFIs in the capital market are regulated and controlled by the Bangladesh Securities and Exchange Commission. Microfinance operations of MFIs are regulated by the Microcredit Regulatory Authority. The regulatory body of the capital market is the Bangladesh Securities and Exchange Commission. The Insurance Development and Regulatory Authority is the regulator of the insurance industry, and the main act covering the activities of this sector is the Insurance Act 2010.

Key Policies for Financial Inclusion

Financial inclusion as a tool for development is covered in several national planning documents, policies, and regulations. Key policies are analyzed here in relation to their attention to the financial inclusion of excluded and vulnerable people. These documents address issues concerning gender equality mainly in the context of women's economic empowerment, though the policies in question rarely specify how they intend to address the intersecting factors that affect women's economic opportunities. Apart from through gender equality, only a few policies cover issues related to the financial inclusion of disadvantaged groups.

Five-Year Plans

Five-year plans are umbrella policy documents for Bangladesh: other policies, programs, and regulations are set up in line with such planning documents. Bangladesh's current 8FYP (July 2020–June 2025) (footnote 6) includes a strategic objective of increasing women's economic participation and benefits. One action plan for achieving this objective is to enhance women's access to and control over productive resources through better access to financial services.

8FYP states that an inclusive financial system is necessary to enhance women's access to and benefits from secure savings, credit, insurance, and payment services. Thus, financial inclusion remains an utmost priority area for women's economic empowerment during its implementation. 8FYP also aims to make DFS/MFS systems more effective in achieving financial inclusion for poor and disadvantaged groups, including PWDs and ethnic minority groups. 8FYP sees financial inclusion platforms like MFIs and MFS as the avenue to distribute social protection benefits more efficiently toward social inclusion.

National Strategy for Social Security

The NSSS, adopted in 2015 (footnote 4), reflects Bangladesh's unwavering commitment to reducing poverty and vulnerability, as it works for increased social and financial inclusion of underprivileged groups. For example, the NSSS aims to strengthen programs for the population of working age, including reducing vulnerability with programs like maternity insurance. Although the NSSS mentions various programs for addressing various needs of other disadvantaged people—including PWDs, ethnic minority groups, and transgender people—it mentions only women's concerns in relation to financial inclusion. There is a huge data gap on financial inclusion of most disadvantaged groups except women.

National Women Development Policy 2011

The National Women Development Policy (NWDP) 2011 includes SME development as a strategy for women's empowerment through their financial inclusion by significantly enhancing microfinance facilities. Despite including programs for girls and women of disadvantaged or ethnic minority background and/or with disability, the policy does not consider how these and other factors combine to create specific and deeper forms of disadvantage for certain groups of women.

National Financial Inclusion Strategy–Bangladesh 2021–2025

The National Financial Inclusion Strategy–Bangladesh (NFIS-B)[30] is intended to serve as a road map for implementing and coordinating all financial inclusion initiatives. It identifies many elements related to the financial infrastructure, regulations, and legislation necessary to achieve its goals. According to this strategy, people excluded from financial services consist of participants in unserved and underserved financial markets who belong to poor and disadvantaged groups; owners of cottage, micro, small, and medium-sized enterprises (CMSMEs); small and marginal farm households; participants in informal sector activities; youth and women belonging to poor households; indigenous people; PWDs; and other disadvantaged groups.

The overall goal of the strategy is to promote the financial inclusion of those excluded from essential financial services. Strategic goals and targets include a goal to *Broaden and Deepen Financial Inclusion of Women, Population Affected by Climate Change and Other Underserved Segments of the Population and Senior Citizens.* To achieve the financial inclusion of women, all regulatory bodies of the finance sector are mandated to develop a separate policy and strategy and to undertake special programs on women's financial inclusion. This goal covers (i) a dedicated focus on providing the needed financial services (saving, credit, payment, investment, insurance) for women individuals and entrepreneurs from both rural and urban areas; (ii) a convenient service delivery channel for women; and (iii) a separate focus on women in DFS. It is also expected that financial service providers will undertake financial literacy programs for women, youth, children, PWDs, third-gender people, and other underserved segments of the population in both urban and remote rural areas.

---

[30]   Financial Institutions Division, Ministry of Finance, Government of Bangladesh. 2021. *National Financial Inclusion Strategy (NFIS-B) 2021–2025.* Dhaka.

The NFIS-B also intends that all regulatory bodies and relevant government agencies formulate target-based specific policies and dedicated programs for financial inclusion for youth; PWDs; third-gender people; children, including those with special needs; elderly and retired persons; overseas migrant workers and diaspora and nonresident Bangladeshis; extremely destitute and underprivileged people such as tea laborers, floating communities, and urban slum dwellers; poor people in remote hilly, forest, coastal, *haor*,[31] or *char*[32] areas, areas with difficult terrain, former enclave areas, sparsely populated areas, and relatively underdeveloped areas with poor infrastructure. The NFIS-B has comprehensive coverage, but its success will depend on whether and how fast diversified financial products and infrastructure are developed that address the specific and gendered needs and priorities of each group listed.

It is also expected under the NFIS-B that technical support and low-cost funding will be sought from development partners to broaden and deepen women's financial inclusion and provide support in ensuring affordable internet and mobile technology to all. However, in implementing this strategy, specific approaches will be necessary for women with different social and personal characteristics. In this context, it will be particularly important to take into consideration women's education levels, and to address the fact that affordable internet and mobile technology cannot reach women if they do not have ownership of a smartphone. Finally, the strategy lacks clear guidelines on how progress will be monitored.

Policies Related to Financial Inclusion of Cottage, Micro, Small, and Medium-Sized Enterprises and Women Entrepreneurs

A large part of financial inclusion strategies for women concentrates on women entrepreneurs, primarily targeted at CMSMEs. The Industrial Policy 2016[33] and the SME Policy 2019[34] aim to promote women's economic empowerment through the development of CMSMEs. They call for easing regulations and creating special provisions to increase the flow of credit to women entrepreneurs. As the relationship between banks and women entrepreneurs presents major constraints to the latter's access to finance, the SME Policy pays attention to the need for coordination between the activities of BB and the SME Foundation (SMEF).[35] In particular, SMEF will organize training for women entrepreneurs to help them understand the availability of, and the process to access, institutional credit. SMEF is also responsible for arranging training for bankers to sensitize them on women entrepreneurs' needs and to increase their knowledge on the demand and supply of finance for SME women entrepreneurs.

---

[31] *Haor* is a wetland ecosystem in the northeastern part of Bangladesh, shaped as a shallow depression, also known as a backswamp (Bangladesh Water Development Board. Haor Flood Management & Livelihood Improvement Project).

[32] *Char* is a tract of land surrounded by the waters of an ocean, sea, lake, or stream; it usually means any accretion in a river course.

[33] Ministry of Industries, Government of Bangladesh. 2016. *Industrial Policy 2016*. Dhaka.

[34] Ministry of Industries, Government of Bangladesh. 2019. *SME Policy 2019*. Dhaka.

[35] The SMEF, the apex institution for SME development, has been working to bring women entrepreneurs into the mainstream through capacity development initiatives in women's chambers of commerce and trade bodies, encouraging bankers to finance women entrepreneurs, and organizing women entrepreneurship conferences, SME product fairs for women entrepreneurs, and other skill-building initiatives. This is a government-supported autonomous organization dedicated to SME development.

The SME Policy 2019 also intends that SMEF will create a *Women Entrepreneur Development Fund* in association with the Finance Division and the Banks and Financial Institutions Division of the Ministry of Finance, the Ministry of Industries, and the Ministry of Women and Children Affairs. The goal of the fund is to provide training and jobs, as well as loans at a reduced interest rate, for women entrepreneurs. According to the SME Policy, the fund should have been created by 2021. However, there is no information available regarding its development.

As already noted, provisions mentioned under CMSME-related regulations and policies are mostly for women; they hardly mention other disadvantaged groups. For example, the SME Policy refers to underprivileged groups in one place only, where it aims to create opportunities to provide financial and business support services to prospective and disadvantaged entrepreneurs. However, there is no elaboration on who these underprivileged people are and what strategies will be adopted.

In 2009, BB made CMSMEs a top priority for rapid development, opening a new department called SME and Special Programs Department (SMESPD) (footnote 18). As mentioned earlier, the gender gap in accessing financial services is 29%, according to the Global Findex Database 2017.[36] To reduce this gap, BB has shifted the policy focus to target the financially excluded and unbanked, especially CMSMEs and women entrepreneurs.[37] BB's development policies for SMEs do not have special provisions for disadvantaged entrepreneurs other than women (special provisions for women are mentioned below). However, in 2015, BB issued a notice to all banks notifying them to take steps to bring disadvantaged groups—including PWDs, ethnic minority groups, and transgender people—under their SME credit facilities.[38] All the same, this did not mention any special provisions for these groups. This implies that such disadvantaged groups will receive only the general provisions intended for any SME, not the additional benefits allowed to women.[39] SMEF has recently declared the extension of credit to PWDs and third-gender SME entrepreneurs.[40]

Other key policy initiatives undertaken by BB to prioritize SME financing for women include the following:

(i)   Banks and NBFIs involved in the refinancing scheme should allocate a minimum refinancing fund of 15% for women entrepreneurs.

(ii)   Banks and NBFIs are instructed to set up a women entrepreneur dedicated desk in each branch, possibly with a female official, to support prospective women entrepreneurs regarding project preparation, the loan application process, and marketing strategies.

(iii)   Banks and NBFIs should extend fresh credit facilities in favor of at least three women entrepreneurs per branch annually.

---

[36]   A. Demirguc-Kunt et al. 2018. *The Global Findex Database 2017: Measuring Financial Inclusion and the Fintech Revolution.* Washington, DC: World Bank.

[37]   Alliance for Financial Inclusion. 2017. *Expanding Women's Financial Inclusion in Bangladesh through MSME Finance Policies.* Kuala Lumpur.

[38]   Bangladesh Bank. 2015. *SMESPD Circular No. 03/2015.* Dhaka.

[39]   These provisions include a lower lending rate compared with for large enterprises and a help desk for SME entrepreneurs. However, women entrepreneurs receive even more benefits.

[40]   *The Business Standard.* 2021. Third Gender Entrepreneurs Too Will Get Stimulus Loans. 27 April.

(iv)   All banks and financial institutions have been instructed to consider authorizing loans to women entrepreneurs up to BDT2.5 million without collateral, but against a personal guarantee. Banks and NBFIs have been advised to consider social security, personal guarantee, and group guarantee, rather than asking for a guarantee of a specific person, for example, a high official, a well-off relative, or a husband.

(v)   BB has initiated a policy of group-based lending of BDT50,000 or above to include large numbers of women microentrepreneurs in SME credit facilities.

In 2019, BB conducted a survey to investigate the impacts of its various financial inclusion measures (footnote 7). The responses from 2,872 persons surveyed reveal that such initiatives have been successful, especially in lifting people's socioeconomic conditions by encouraging them to save, improving access to finance, easing the process to receive domestic and foreign remittances, and encouraging them to adopt an insurance policy. However, the survey pointed out that banks and financial institutions should limit the required documents for opening bank accounts, as these are a significant barrier to financial inclusion. One way of resolving this could be through introducing e-KYC, at least for MFS.

Regulations on Mobile Financial Services and e-KYC

All regulations related to providing MFS, as well as the e-KYC Guidelines, support financial inclusion. BB has instructed all MFS companies to open accounts for garment workers and receivers of government subsidies, stipends, and scholarships and to allow them to withdraw their money at a subsidized cash-out fee (footnote 18). An additional positive move is that the application form for e-KYC has the provision for male, female, and transgender identification.

4 Key Gender and Social Inclusion Issues and Gaps in the Finance Sector

As discussed, financial inclusion is an effective tool to ensure inclusive and sustainable economic development. This is also because financial access facilitates day-to-day living and helps families and businesses plan for unexpected long-term emergencies (footnote 36). Furthermore, financial inclusion is a way to increase women's access to economic and productive resources. Thus, it expands their autonomy and social networks, leading to increased voice and bargaining power in the household and enhanced mobility and leadership in the public domain. Financial inclusion of other disadvantaged groups in society can generate similar benefits.

This section looks at the extent and nature of gaps in financial inclusion in terms of GESI. We have already noted that provisions for financial inclusion, at both policy and institutional level, mostly try to address gender gaps, while failing to understand what other dimensions, except that of gender, are responsible for women's limited financial inclusion. Information on the broader context of social inclusion of other disadvantaged groups is also inadequate. Data on the financial inclusion of other disadvantaged groups is very limited. Some national-level data exists on the number of households with disabled members and types of disabilities, but nothing on their financial inclusion.

Given the size of the informal economy in Bangladesh, and the concentration of women in the sector, it is useful to articulate this as a broader challenge within the country context. While the informal economy plays a big role in employment, such work can be transient in nature, and its informality can limit the inclusion of individuals and small businesses in the formal financial systems of Bangladesh.

State of Gender Equality and Social Inclusion Gaps in the Finance Sector

According to the 2017 Global Findex Database, 65% of men in Bangladesh have bank accounts against only 35.8% of women (footnote 37). This means that around 64% of women in Bangladesh are unbanked. Thus, the gender gap is 29 percentage points or 45% (Table 3), one of the largest in the world, according to the same source. Compared with the 2014 Global Findex Database, by 2017, the percentage of adults with financial accounts had risen from 31% to 50%, while the gender gap had worsened from 20 percentage points to 29 percentage points. In the 2017 database, there is no information on the nature of financial inclusion of other disadvantaged groups. This was also not present in earlier Global Findex reports.

A tracker survey by Financial Inclusion Insights (FII), which provides a wide range of evidence on DFS, has more information on differences in financial inclusion based on 2018 data.[41] This report highlights that women remain financially underserved compared with men, based on differences in access of financial services.

---

[41] Financial Inclusion Insights. 2019. *Bangladesh, Wave 6 Report, Sixth Annual FII Tracker Survey 2018*. Washington, DC.

Table 3: The Gender Gap on Some Indicators of Financial Behavior
According to the Global Findex Database 2017

Particulars	Male (% of Adult Males)	Female (% of Adult Females)	Gender Gap (%)
Ownership of bank account	65	35.8	45
Borrowed any money in past year	41	37	10
Debit card ownership	9	4	56
Saved at a financial institution	10	10	0
Saved to start, operate, or expand a business	9	7	22
Used internet to buy something online in past year	1	2	−100

Source: Global Findex Database 2017.

The FII survey covered 6,000 adults and found that 47% of the respondents were financially included. It also mentioned that 17% of the respondents had a registered mobile money account. Mobile money was the preferred digital payment channel to buy goods and services from merchants. Out of 3,466 women respondents, 10% had MFS accounts; this was 24% for the 2,534 surveyed men, making the gender gap in MFS account holding 58%. Moreover, less than 1% of all MFS agents in Bangladesh are women.[42] The gender disparity in registered bank users was 33%. Various financial inclusion indicators mentioned in the FII show that women lag behind men in almost all cases except for registered users of NBFIs (which also includes MFIs) (Table 4) (footnote 41).

Female registered NBFI users outnumber registered male users because NBFIs include MFIs, which mainly target women as beneficiaries. However, gender gaps exist in key predictors of DFS adoption.[43] According to the FII survey, only 32% of women utilize digital platforms, against 56% of males, which translates to a 43% gender gap in accessing a digital payment or transfer.

Although the gender gap for ownership of any cell phone was 14%, according to the FII survey, there was a gender difference of 47% in smartphone ownership. A more recent survey by the Global System for Mobile Communications (GSMA) (2020)[44] states that mobile phone (any type) ownership among men is 86% and among women is 61%; thus, the gender gap is 29%. According to this source, the situation has improved: the respective 2019 figures were 86% for males and 58% for females, and the gender gap was 33%. GSMA underlines that mobile phones in low- and middle-income countries are the primary means of internet access, and women's lower rate of smartphone ownership means a lower level of internet use. According to this database, the gender gap is 52% in mobile internet use, with 33% of men and 16% of women using the internet.

---

[42] International Finance Corporation. 2018. *Closing the Gender Gap: Opportunities for the Women's Mobile Financial Services Market in Bangladesh.* Washington, DC.

[43] These indicators include possessing necessary ID, phone access, SIM card ownership, texting ability, financial literacy, and financial numeracy.

[44] Global System for Mobile Communications. 2020. *Connected Women: The Mobile Gender Gap Report 2020.*

Table 4: Gender Gaps on Selected Indicators of Financial Inclusion, 2018

Particular	Male (% of Adult Males)	Female (% of Adult Females)	Gender Gap (%)
Registered users of banks	30	20	33
Registered users of MFS	24	10	58
Registered users of NBFI[a]	20	27	−35
Own or access mobile phone (any type)	91	78	14
Own smartphone	30	16	47
Have necessary ID	87	84	3
Own SIM card	88	70	20
Able to send and receive text messages	55	39	29
Financial literacy	33	24	27
Financial numeracy	87	79	9
Accessed a digital payment or transfer	56	32	43

ID = identification, MFS = mobile financial services, NBFI = nonbanking financial institution, SIM = subscriber identity module.

[a] Financial Inclusion Insights considers microfinance institutions, insurance, and NBFIs under one umbrella of NBFI.

Source: Financial Inclusion Insights. 2019. *Bangladesh, Wave 6 Report, Sixth Annual FII Tracker Survey 2018*. Washington, DC.

There are differences in decision-making within financially included and financially excluded segments of the population that perpetuate a persistent gender gap.[45] While 77% of financially included male respondents have household spending decision-making power, only 44% of the financially included female respondents have the same authority (Table 5). The gender gap is higher for financially excluded respondents for both men and women.

Although we get a good range of information on gender gaps in both the Global Findex Database 2017 and the FII 2019, these reports do not provide any information on the financial exclusion of other disadvantaged groups. Thus, it is essential to note a significant data dearth in the global database regarding GESI aspects of financial services. Disaggregated data could greatly help in formulating effective policies and programs specifically for their financial inclusion.

---

[45]   The FII survey tracks economic empowerment through a set of four indicators that measure the influence, voice, agency, and control adults have in their household financial activities measured on a five-point scale. For a woman, ability to have bargaining power in her household and to influence joint decisions on household spending is empowering. Ability to voice disagreement within her household and to have the agency or power to make household decisions is tied to a greater sense of well-being. Control over her own finances empowers a woman to decide what to do with her own money without relying on input from family members.

Table 5: Comparison of Gender Gap among Financially Included
and Financially Excluded Respondents

Empowerment Indicator	Explanation of Empowerment Indicators	Financially Included (% of Respondents)		Financially Excluded (% of Respondents)	
		Male	Female	Male	Female
Influence	I have most/almost all influence on final decisions on household spending	77	44	60	32
Voice	I am somewhat/very likely to voice disagreement with a spending decision	81	69	68	56
Agency	I am somewhat/very involved in deciding how to spend household income	88	76	72	57
Control	I make the final decision on how my money is spent or saved	89	72	78	59

Source: Financial Inclusion Insights. 2019. *Bangladesh, Wave 6 Report, Sixth Annual FII Tracker Survey 2018*. Washington, DC.

Gender Equality and Social Inclusion Gaps in the Financing of Cottage, Micro, Small, and Medium-Sized Enterprises

Labor force participation of women in Bangladesh has increased over time, from 16% in 1995/96 to 36% in 2016.[46] Among the women included in the labor force, only around 12% are listed as entrepreneurs. Among the 7.8 million businesses in Bangladesh, 99.93% are CMSMEs.[47] The percentage of women-owned businesses, however, is only 7.21%. Moreover, women account for only 17% of individuals that CMSMEs employ.[48] This low participation rate results from several economic and cultural barriers, but one of the most significant challenges facing women entrepreneurs in Bangladesh is access to finance (footnote 37).

Data provided in the Quarterly Statement on SME Loan Disbursement by BB shows that only 6.6% of borrowers in FY2019/20 were women (Table 6). A similar situation is noted for the number of loans obtained by women borrowers: only around 3.3% of total micro, small, and medium-sized enterprise (MSME) loans go to women entrepreneurs.[49] Moreover, the loan size per MSME female borrower is almost half the average amount obtained by male MSME borrowers.

BB maintains (through banks and NBFIs) two refinance funds dedicated only to women entrepreneurs, under its Small Enterprise Refinance Scheme. Although there is a general loan disbursement part under this scheme, the larger part of the total loan goes to women entrepreneurs. In 2020, out of BDT45.7 billion disbursed from this fund, BDT33.49 billion (73.16%) went to women entrepreneurs.[50]

---

[46]   Bangladesh Bureau of Statistics. 2017. *Labor Force Survey 2016/17*. Dhaka.

[47]   Bangladesh Bureau of Statistics. 2013. *Economic Census*. Dhaka.

[48]   According to the Economic Census 2013, 24.5 million people were engaged in CMSMEs.

[49]   C. D. Shoma. 2019. Financing Female Entrepreneurs in Cottage, Micro, Small, and Medium Enterprises: Evidence from the Financial Sector in Bangladesh 2010–2018. *Asia and the Pacific Policy Studies*. 6(3). pp. 397–416.

[50]   Bangladesh Bank. 2020. *Information on Entrepreneur's Refinanced Under Small Enterprise Refinance Scheme.*

Table 6: Gender Gap in Small and Medium-Sized Enterprise Credit in Terms of Number of Borrowers, Amount of Borrowing, and Average Loan Size, 2019/20

Number of MSME Borrowers and Share of Female Borrowers			
Number of Total MSME Borrowers	Number of Female MSME Borrowers	Number of Male MSME Borrowers	% of Female Borrowers in Total MSME Borrowers
662,602	43,726	618,876	6.6
Amount of Loan Taken by Different Borrowers and Share of Female Entrepreneurs in Disbursed Loan			
Total Disbursed Amount to MSMEs (BDT billion)	Amount of Loan Disbursed to Female Entrepreneurs (BDT billion)	Amount of Loan Disbursed to Male Entrepreneurs (BDT billion)	Share of Female Entrepreneurs in Total Disbursed Loan Amount (%)
1,625.9	49.44	1,476.5	3.24
Loan Size			
Loan Size per Borrower Among All MSME Borrowers (BDT million)	Loan Size per Female Borrower (BDT million)	Loan Size per Male Borrower (BDT million)	
2.3	1.13	2.39	

BDT = Bangladesh taka; MSMEs = micro, small, and medium-sized enterprises; SMEs = small and medium-sized enterprises.

Note: Excludes cottage industry.

Source: Calculated based on Bangladesh Bank. Quarterly Statement of SME Loan Disbursement.

It is to be noted that BB does not provide information on the financial inclusion of other disadvantaged SME entrepreneurs. A 2015 BB notice (footnote 38) notified all banks and financial institutions to take steps to bring PWDs, those from ethnic communities, and disadvantaged women entrepreneurs under their SME credit facilities. However, BB itself does not have a system of collecting relevant information. Thus, there is no monitoring of the implementation of this notice.

Reasons for Financial Exclusion

General Perspectives

Despite the substantial expansion of bank branches and the increase in the membership of MFIs and other financial institutions, much of the country's adult population remains financially excluded, according to a BB survey in 2019 (footnote 7). The main reasons for financial exclusion are given as poor physical access or banking infrastructure; high requirement for minimum balance; inadequate financial literacy or education; lack of proper documentation (including ID cards, wage slips, proof of domicile, and reference letter); lack of initiatives of banks and financial institutions; low level of technological infrastructure; lack of suitable product structure of banks and MFIs; low income; opportunity cost (time and money) of getting financial services; high cost of products, especially, in the case of MFIs; and absence of credit bureau and insurance of MFI borrowers. While both men and women face these barriers, the obstacles appear to be more difficult for women get past. However, it remains unclear how gender intersects with other characteristics to contribute to and aggravate this situation for specific groups of women. Unfortunately, the survey report does not provide any information on other disadvantaged groups.

In the case of financial inclusion for insurance, the same survey notes a meager rate of insurance exposure. Only 14% of respondents (out of 2,872) had an insurance policy. The adoption rate was found to be higher for banked respondents: 17% had an insurance policy compared with only 8% for unbanked respondents. The main reasons for not having insurance were lack of knowledge about insurance policies, lack of trust in insurance companies, and not feeling the need for an insurance policy. Though these reasons are common for all respondents (male and female), lower financial inclusion of women can be expected in all types of financial products.

Gender Perspectives on Financial Exclusion

Female MSME entrepreneurs face different obstacles in both society and financial institutions, and this constrains their access to finance. These problems can be divided into two groups: demand-side problems—in other words, the sociocultural barriers facing women, which prevent them from participating in economic and business activities; and supply-side challenges, which affect their ability to access finance.[51]

Demand-side problems facing women, especially entrepreneurs, include difficulties in arranging loan-related papers; lack of knowledge and information regarding procedures in banks; lack of business or technical experience; lack of overall knowledge regarding business opportunities and credit facilities; hesitation in applying for a loan from a commercial bank; and considering interest rates to be high. A notable obstacle for women in general and for female entrepreneurs in particular in obtaining loans and other financial support is related to their inability to meet collateral requirements, especially those linked to land and other property ownership. While in Bangladesh many laws grant women the right to own and inherit land, in practice, they are largely excluded from ownership, and their access to and control over other assets are severely limited.[52] This is exacerbated by the fact that collateral requirements for credit are at times higher for small businesses owned by women than for those owned by men (footnote 49).

Other demand-sides reasons may include issues related to women's ownership of and access to mobile phones and SIM cards, discussed earlier. In this context, the FII 2019 survey (footnote 41) also identified skills shortage as another reason for financial exclusion among women. Skills include the ability to text, financial literacy and numeracy, and financial management. Women also do not have confidence in their proficiency in financial management.

---

51   A. Eusuf et al. 2017. *The Shared Roles of the Central Bank, Commercial Banks and Women Chambers in Promoting Innovative Financing Models for Women-Led SMEs.* The Asia Foundation and Centre on Budget and Policy.

52   A. de Pinto et al. 2020. Women's Empowerment and Farmland Allocations in Bangladesh: Evidence of a Possible Pathway to Crop Diversification. *Climatic Change.* 163. pp. 1025–1043.

One considerable supply-side reason for financial exclusion is the location of bank branches. In most cases (especially for PCBs), branches are in urban or semi-urban areas. This creates obstacles for women living in rural areas, given their time poverty[53] and social norms preventing women from leaving their home for long periods. Moreover, the limited number of ATM booths[54] means women have to travel to distant urban places to access cash. There is also a lack of female-friendly banking products. Only a few banks (like BRAC Bank, City Bank, and Dutch–Bangla Bank) provide a range of female-focused products.[55] Green Delta Insurance has a female-focused insurance policy called *Nibedita Comprehensive Insurance Policy for Women.*

Supply-side difficulties specifically for women entrepreneurs include absence of a proper policy framework and negative attitudes among commercial banks. For instance, in many banks, staff members are under the impression that it is male family members who operate the business, even when the license is in the woman's name (footnote 51). A survey of 1,510 women entrepreneurs by SMEF in 2017[56] found that 81.3% of respondents were running their business activities independently. However, these women entrepreneurs mostly lack proper accounting and inventory management, and they consider collateral requirements for large-scale loans to be a constraint.

According to a report published by United Nations Capital Development Fund in 2018,[57] out of the 1.3 million micro-merchants in Bangladesh, only 7.2% are women (micro-merchants here refer to microentrepreneurs). The report suggests some common characteristics for the women: (i) have no formal education; (ii) run an informal business (few have a trade license); (iii) obtain loans from MFIs that traditionally focus on serving men; (iv) have low access to bank accounts and MFS; and (v) have mobile phones, but limited internet access. Thus, this report confirms the widespread gender gaps in financial inclusion.

Finally, in Bangladesh, financial institutions do not have reliable sex-disaggregated management information systems. Lack of such data means financial institutions cannot establish the business case for serving low-income women or have a clear understanding of the female market, especially women's financial needs and behavior.

---

[53]   Limited time available after completing their daily household chores.

[54]   Not enough bank booths are available in their vicinity, though the number is rising. In 2019, every 100,000 adults in Bangladesh had 9.39 ATMs (World Bank. Data).

[55]   In most cases, the products are accessible only by women, whose needs or priorities they are designed to meet.

[56]   SME Foundation. 2017. *Women Entrepreneurs in SMEs: Bangladesh Perspective 2017.*

[57]   United Nations Capital Development Fund. 2019. *Landscape Assessment of Retail Micro-Merchants in Bangladesh. Micro-Merchant Research into Action Series.*

The Female Workforce in the Finance Sector

Gender equality in the finance sector can also be seen in terms of participation of women in the sector workforce. Only 15% of the workforce in the banking sector in Bangladesh is female. FCBs have the highest share of female employees, at 31.96%, followed by PCBs, which employ 16,076 female employees, or 18.33% of their workforce (Table 7). Women are also lagging in top management posts: women hold only around 8.4% of the top-level positions and are a minority in board member positions (13.34%) (Table 8).

Table 7: Female Workforce in the Scheduled Banks of Bangladesh

Type of Bank	Number of Female Employees	Number of Male Employees	Share of Female Employees (%)
State-owned banks	7,262	42,788	16.97
Specialized commercial banks	1,495	10,670	14.01
Private commercial banks	16,076	87,711	18.33
Foreign banks	938	2,935	31.96
All banks	**25,771**	**144,104**	**15.171**

Source: Bangladesh Bank. 2019. *Gender Equality Report of Banks and FI, January–June*. Dhaka.

Table 8: Female Employees and Board Members in the Banking Sector in Bangladesh

Type of Bank	Women Members of the Board (%)	Women in High-Level Positions (%)	Women in Medium-Level Positions (%)	Women in Entry-Level Positions (%)
State-owned banks	14.29	9.74	15.1	14.52
Specialized commercial banks	13	6.73	12.13	12.57
Private commercial banks	14	7.15	15.51	15.97
Foreign banks	7.69	20.34	20.6	26.9
All banks	**13.34**	**8.49**	**15.3**	**15.48**

Source: Bangladesh Bank. 2019. *Gender Equality Report of Banks and FI, January–June*. Dhaka.

A survey of 4,000 women (2,000 MFS users and 2,000 MFS nonusers) documented by the International Finance Corporation (IFC) (footnote 42) noted a clear preference for female agents among women users of these services, with 52% of respondents answering in the affirmative. Respondents believe that female agents will behave in a friendlier way and provide a superior service. However, women make up only 1% of MFS agents. As many MFS account holders are female, including many ready-made garment (RMG) workers, it will be beneficial for MFS providers to appoint more female agents. Female clients are more comfortable conducting their banking with female employees. As such, more female employees in a bank may attract more women to be account holders, take out loans, and create business for the bank.

ADB conducted a gender audit of several partner banks in different countries (including Bangladesh)[58] under its Trade Finance Program[59] to determine whether partner banks' human resources policies could be enhanced to bring more women in banking. The results reveal that senior management and boards in several banks strongly consider the need to improve the gender balance in their organization, for societal and economic growth. The audit notes that, in Bangladesh, maternity benefit policy practices in banks are good. However, the law requires staff to rotate bank branches every 3 years; this is a specific issue for women with children, who cannot relocate.

Financial Exclusion of Other Disadvantaged People

PWDs do not have full access to leading lending sources in Bangladesh because of discrimination and accessibility barriers. Discrimination is present in terms of attitudes on the part of representatives and staff of financial institutions, including MFIs, in relation to the non-provision of information and to refusing offers of loan for lack of confidence in ability to repay. Other barriers can be in the form of lack of facilities for those with limited mobility or with hearing or sight impairments. Prejudices and tangible obstacles lead to the persistent exclusion of PWDs from financial services (footnote 8).

Research on the financial exclusion of, for example, transgender people, both as providers and as clients, is scarce. The policies summarized earlier do indicate that there is awareness in the country of the financial exclusion experienced by rural and other disadvantaged groups. However, except for women and, to a lesser extent, PWDs, policy documents may have strategies to address the financial exclusion of other disadvantaged groups—for example, older and transgender people—but remain silent about necessary practical measures.

---

[58]   ADB. 2018. *Boosting Gender Equality through ADB Trade Finance Partnerships*. Manila.

[59]   As part of the ADB Gender Equality and Women's Empowerment Operational Plan 2013–2020, the Trade Finance Program, in partnership with the Sustainable Development and Climate Change Department, launched the first private sector project on institutional gender equality with the Trade Finance Program's partner banks in November 2016. Forty banks from nine of the Trade Finance Program's 21 countries of operation were invited to join the initiative and 20 participated.

5 Some Good Practices and Lessons Learned

This section summarizes some good practices in financial inclusion. The analysis focuses mainly on the financial inclusion of women, as information on this topic is more readily available. More specifically, it discusses several initiatives implemented by different organizations to address the gender gap in the finance sector and, later, how financial technology companies can transform the experience of financial solutions for women.

Women-Focused Products by Banks

Women-focused products offered by different banks cover bank account services with higher deposit rates for women; debit and credit card facilities with special privileges; low-cost loan facilities for women entrepreneurs; business support advisory services; and consumer loans at preferential interest rates (Appendix).

The City Bank Ltd has a women-focused banking solution called *City Alo*. Other than financial products, such as savings accounts, current accounts, and different types of retails loans, *City Alo* in collaboration with the North-South University (a private university in Bangladesh) offers a certification course for female entrepreneurs to expand their business. BRAC Bank Ltd also has a women-only banking product lineup, called *Tara*. *Tara's* savings account gives more return than any other regular savings account. Women can also avail themselves of debit and credit card facilities, allowing them to reduce visits to bank branches. In addition, the annual fee for a debit card is waived for the first year. The user can get a monthly cashback offer on every purchase from a grocery store, which encourages use of the debit card. *Tara* credit cards are offered with a lifetime waiver of a 30% annual fee, with an additional 10% discount if the card is bundled with any retail loan products.[60] *Tara* account holders also have preferential interest rates, loan approval in the shortest time, a 50% discount on processing fees, and maximum loan tenure.

Lanka Bangla Finance Ltd, IDLC Finance Limited, Eastern Bank Limited, and Dutch–Bangla Bank have their own women-focused banking solutions. These institutions have SME credit programs especially for women entrepreneurs that help them access loans. In most cases, women banking officers handle these products. All these women-focused services mitigate the information gaps facing women in becoming entrepreneurs, increase their access to credit, and encourage them to be linked with formal financial services.

Again, there are no equivalent products for other disadvantaged groups such as PWDs, ethnic minorities, and transgender people.

---

[60] The first-year waiver is for debit cards, the lifetime 30% annual fee waiver is for credit cards.

Women-Focused Insurance Products

Green Delta Insurance has a women-focused insurance policy called *Nibedita Comprehensive Insurance Policy for Women*. This aims to provide economic security to women facing accidental death or permanent or temporary physical injury owing to an accident, childbirth, riot, strike, civil commotion, or a natural hazard; a trauma allowance in response to rape, bullying, robbery, or an acid attack; and loss or damage to household goods and/or personal effects as a result of fire or natural hazard. With this product, women receive more attention and a greater level of information from the provider, and this encourages them to obtain insurance coverage, reducing the gender gap in insurance services.

Green Delta Insurance also has a weather-based crop insurance policy, supporting farmers in different parts of the country. As agriculture is the primary source of women's employment, crop insurance can help in their economic empowerment by minimizing risks and reducing loss. Although many women do not own land, they may utilize household land (usually owned by a male relative) to produce vegetables and other crops and may have some control over this income. Therefore, crop insurance can serve even women who are without land ownership.

Some Practices under Mobile Financial Services

An innovative initiative in MFS by *bKash* has contributed significantly to addressing the gender gap in financial inclusion.[61] In 2016, around 100 rural women agro-input sellers had the opportunity to become *bKash* agents, giving them a new income source.[62] *bKash* also partnered with *Shakti Foundation for Disadvantaged Women* to allow the beneficiaries of the foundation to receive a loan directly to their bKash account and let them pay the installments via their bKash wallet.[63] More than 350,000 RMG workers (the majority are women) received wages through their *bKash* wallet as of October 2019.

A pilot project by BRAC led to over 150,000 female clients paying small amounts into monthly savings using *bKash*,[64] encouraging the financial inclusion of women. Through support from IFC, over 70,000 female workers received their wage payment in their MFS account between 2016 and 2018. This enabled beneficiaries of BRAC to save, send money, and make payments safely. It also reduced their time poverty. Many RMG workers family live in rural areas, dependent on their income. Previously, without a bank account, it was difficult for them to send money home promptly.

Looking at specific financial activities, Hernandez has also found that Bangladeshi women do not use mobile money either through their own registered accounts or through the accounts of other people.[65]

---

[61]   bKash. 2019. World Bank Group Excited over Role of bKash RMG Sector's Wage Digitization. 4 November.

[62]   bKash. 2016. bKash Joins Hands with USAID-Funded Agro-Input Retailers Network to Increase Incomes of Rural Women. 1 June.

[63]   bKash. 2018. Shakti Foundation, bKash Sign Deal to Facilitate Loan Disbursement and Repayment. 5 August.

[64]   S. Abed. 2018. Bridging the Digital Gender Divide in Financial Inclusion. Blog, 16 October.

[65]   K. Hernandez. 2019. Barriers to Digital Services Adoption in Bangladesh. *K4D Helpdesk Report Series*. No. 573. Brighton: Institute of Development Studies.

They are also less likely to engage in more advanced digital finance activities than men (2% versus 5%). A policy brief by the Asian Development Bank Institute (ADBI) explains how technological advancement in financial services or DFS may play an essential role in bridging the gender gap in financial inclusion. If financial technologies are more advanced, easier to use, and more readily accessible, they could increase the formalization of women's transactions, protect and educate them against fraud and unfair transactions, and empower them by making them agents of their financial futures.[66]

MFS have great potential to increase women's financial inclusion, but this has not yet been fully realized. Women are less likely to be mobile phone owners and internet users than men globally. Moreover, women and girls are less likely to use digital technologies across all activities, including social media, surfing the internet, accessing entertainment, playing games, instant messaging, banking, e-mail, and studying. Therefore, mobile money adoption alone does not guarantee gender equality in finance (footnote 65).

Gender Equality and Social Inclusion in ADB-Supported Finance Sector Projects in Bangladesh

The Country Partnership Strategy (CPS) of Bangladesh 2021–2025 (footnote 1) commits to harmonizing ADB Operational Priority 1 (OP1): Addressing Remaining Poverty and Reducing Inequalities—under which ADB supports the Sustainable Development Goal agenda to tackle poverty and inequality and leave no one behind;[67] and Operational Priority 2 (OP2): Accelerating Progress in Gender Equality in Asia and the Pacific—under which ADB will expand integrated support for women entrepreneurs and women-led SMEs through better access to finance, the adoption of new technologies, and policy and institutional reforms.[68] The CPS also offers further guidance to address more consistently and in a more harmonized manner both gender inequality and social inclusion across all sectors, including in finance sector projects. This is because the CPS explicitly commits to accelerate gender equality and social inclusion and *"harmonize OP1 and OP2 priorities to expand focus from gender equality to gender equality and social inclusion (GESI)"* (footnote 1).

In line with the above, supporting *access to finance* has been added as a key outcome for ADB's Bangladesh operations. As per the CPS and other country documents, ADB will contribute to foster through the finance sector projects (i) a more inclusive finance sector; (ii) higher private investment; and (iii) increased women's participation in education and employment.[69] This will be reflected in upcoming loans and projects in the sector and will consider various dimensions of exclusion and vulnerability, including gender; age (older people, youth, and children); disability; social identities; sexual and gender identities; geographic location; and income status. In the finance sector, ADB is committed to improving the business environment and increasing access to financing for microenterprises, including for CMSMEs, with an earmark of 28% total bank credit increased of at least 10% for SMEs led by women (footnote 1).

66   ADB. 2019. Closing the Gender Gap in Financial Inclusion Through Fintech. *Policy Brief*. No. 2019-3 (April). Manila.
67   ADB. 2019. *Strategy 2030 Operational Plan for Priority 1 Addressing Remaining Poverty and Reducing Inequalities, 2019–2024*. Manila.
68   ADB. 2019. *Strategy 2030 Operational Plan for Priority 2 Accelerating Progress in Gender Equality, 2019–2024*. September. Manila.
69   ADB. 2019. *Country Operations Business Plan, Bangladesh 2020–2022*. Manila.

In addition, to enhance access to essential services and financial inclusion, in the next 5 years ADB will increase the number of active MFS accounts annually by at least 5%, with an earmark of 10% for women and disadvantaged groups (footnote 1). Involvement of excluded and vulnerable groups will be facilitated in the design of projects to accelerate gender equality and improve social inclusion. Upcoming loans such as the Post COVID-19 Small-Scale Employment Creation Fund (2021) will aim at providing access to finance not only to women, but also to disadvantaged groups such as returnee migrants, youth, and rural microbusiness owners. The pipeline also includes additional financing for the SME Development Facility in 2022, where technical support for transgender groups is envisioned, and the second policy-based Sustainable Economic Recovery Program in 2023, which will focus on policy-level changes for women and other disadvantaged groups.

As of December 2020, ADB had seven active finance sector-related projects only for Bangladesh (no regional projects considered).[70] The respective project documents explicitly mention the gender mainstreaming classification of each project, according to ADB's Gender Mainstreaming Categories (ADB 2013).[71] However, it should be noted that ADB's Gender Mainstreaming Categories were updated in 2021.[72] Here, we discuss the projects that have the potential to achieve or that already have achieved gender-related outcomes.

The **Microenterprise Development Project** and **Microenterprise Development Project—Additional Financing** are two active projects with gender equity themes, directly addressing gender equality and women's empowerment, with the second as an additional finance to the earlier one. Both these projects opt for inclusive economic growth through promoting microenterprise development initiatives. They support improving microenterprise access to finance through the DFI *PKSF* and its POs. The activities in the gender action plans (GAPs) aim to provide women with access to mobile-based finance applications. Under the Microenterprise Development Project, which started in 2018, a total of 11,146 microenterprise borrowers, of whom at least 95% are female from three POs, enrolled in a mobile-based microenterprise finance application and received training. The enrollment of more microenterprise borrowers from three new POs is underway and will be completed in 2022.[73]

---

[70]   Here, the finance sector projects refer to those projects that ADB has categorized as "finance sector projects" in the online project information database. These projects are (i) the Microenterprise Development Project—Additional Financing (ADB Project No. 51269-002); (ii) the Microenterprise Development Project (ADB Project No. 51269-001); (iii) Sustainable Projects in the Textile and Garment Sector (ADB Project No. 50197-001); (iv) the Second SME Development Project (ADB Project No. 36200-023); (v) Sustainable Projects (ADB Project No. 49074-001); (vi) the Third Public–Private Infrastructure Development Facility—Tranche 1 (ADB Project No. 42180-018); and (vii) the Third Public–Private Infrastructure Development Facility (ADB Project No. 42180-016). The first four projects mentioned here include some financial inclusion aspects; the other three are mostly finance sector projects for infrastructure development and do not have direct financial inclusion components. Therefore, we discuss gender outcomes of only the first four.

[71]   ADB. 2013. *Understanding and Applying Gender Mainstreaming Categories.* Manila. This document classifies any ADB-funded program or project into any of the following gender mainstreaming categories: (i) Category I: gender equity theme. This is used when the project outcome directly addresses gender equality and/or women's empowerment; (ii) Category II: effective gender mainstreaming. The project outcome does not specifically address gender equality or women's empowerment, but the outputs are designed to deliver tangible benefits to women by directly improving access to services, opportunities, and infrastructure and/or enhancing their voices and rights; (iii) Category III: some gender elements. It is unlikely to directly improve women's access to services, opportunities, and voice, but significant efforts were made to include some gender features to enhance benefits for women; (iv) Category IV: no gender elements. This is used when a project does not include any gender design features.

[72]   ADB. 2021. *Guidelines for Gender Mainstreaming Categories of ADB Projects.* Manila.

[73]   As mentioned in the project documents available online.

Under **Sustainable Projects in the Textile and Garment Sector** (approved in 2016), ADB provides a 5-year *senior unsecured term loan* to a commercial bank. The commercial bank uses the fund to support socially and environmentally sustainable projects in the textile and garments sector. The project is categorized as *effective gender mainstreaming*. The GAP includes several subprojects to improve facilities and working conditions for women in the RMG industry. The GAP has several gender design features, including day care, safety, and health clinics, to be incorporated into operations by the RMG factory sub-borrowers. However, this project does not contain women's financial inclusion features. This is a serious gap, as financial inclusion of garment workers is necessary to reduce their time poverty and increase their control over their earnings. DFS would be very relevant, especially for salaries and other transfers. Any such project should include the supply of low-cost smartphones to workers for this purpose, and to prevent women losing control over their earnings as their salary is often transferred to their husband's mobile account.

The purpose of the Second SME Development Project is to enhance access to bank finance and financial services of MSMEs with special attention to women entrepreneurs. All participating financial institutions must dedicate at least 15% of the sub-loans to women SME sub-borrowers to meet the project target of $20 million. In addition, women entrepreneurs' needs were to be incorporated in the design and development of incubation centers to strengthen the capacity of SME entrepreneurs to access bank financing. The GAP of the project has four output goals: increased medium- to long-term credit to non-urban areas (including SME clusters and Bangladesh Small and Cottage Industries Corporation estates); strengthened capacity of SME entrepreneurs to access bank financing; enhanced managerial and technical capacity of SME entrepreneurs and staff dealing with them; and improved access to bank finance and financial services of women-led SMEs. All these goals have gender equality implications, and the last one deals only with women. In addition, this output aims to provide training on legal literacy and financial literacy, two areas that present significant obstacles for women entrepreneurs. However, only two training workshops per year were envisaged in the GAP.

The evaluation report of the ADB-funded and completed **SME Development Project** (2009–2013) notes that, compared with the situation in the 2010 baseline, implementation had led to an increase in the number of loans to women-owned SMEs of more than 26%, while the amount lent had increased by 23% (from all the different refinancing schemes).[74] Under the project, more than 4.5% of the overall SME loans under the refinancing scheme were granted to women SMEs. The project also enhanced the capacity of women entrepreneurs and associations to fully access the financial resources earmarked for women-led SMEs. The financial inclusion of women in terms of credit facilities came through some contributory factors: (i) inclusion of a technical assistance (TA) element that focused specifically on women entrepreneurs; (ii) single-source selection of the Bangladesh Women Chamber of Commerce and Industry (BWCCI) as the implementing agency for the TA; (iii) a proactive role for ADB in managing the project; and (iv) a rapport established between the Ministry of Finance, BB, ADB, and BWCCI. These findings imply that future projects to support the SME sector should include these contributory factors. Moreover, the financial inclusion of other disadvantaged groups should be considered in ADB-funded projects.

---

[74]   ADB. 2015. *Gender Equality Results, Case Study: Bangladesh. Small and Medium-Sized Enterprise Development Project*. Manila.

6 Looking Ahead: Issues and Opportunities to Consider for Gender Equality and Social Inclusion in ADB Operations

The previous section looked at women-focused products offered by banks (special savings and credit accounts, loans, debt, and credit card facilities), women-focused insurance policies and services, and pioneering MFS. It also looked at a few of ADB's projects in Bangladesh with the potential to achieve, or that already have achieved, gender-related outcomes. Already, all targeted investments across ADB projects aim to mainstream activities to support gender equality, but they do not necessarily include social inclusion issues. Projects reviewed range from interventions that provide women with access to mobile-based finance applications to those to improve the capacity of SME entrepreneurs to access bank financing, especially women-led SMEs. In some cases, projects have included substantive gender design features, such as the provision of childcare, safety, and health clinics for factory workers, but not women's financial inclusion features.

This section examines initiatives that feature critical GESI issues and opportunities that ADB could learn from and could consider in the design of its finance sector operations.

Initiatives to Enhance Entrepreneurship among Women and Other Excluded Groups

This report has made it clear that a critical way of facilitating access to financial resources for women comes through supporting microenterprises and SMEs owned and managed by them. One way of supporting women entrepreneurs is to provide them with easily accessible information on (i) business and credit opportunities, (ii) documents required to avail themselves of such opportunities, and (iii) ways to reduce the time and cost involved in accessing financial services. The guarantor requirement is a big constraint for women entrepreneurs in SMEs when applying for bank credit: many banks ask for at least two guarantors (though one is enough for a collateral-free loan). Alternative methods could include eliminating this need for a personal guarantee to receive credit. This may mean credit is allowed for a group, or women chambers providing guarantees.[75]

---

[75] A Bangladesh Bank regulation (*SMESPD Circular No. 2, 29-6-2017*) on conditions for loan application by SME women entrepreneurs mentions six types of collateral or guarantee possibilities, from which banks may ask for one or more types depending on the size and type of the loan: (i) hypothecation (inventory of products, machinery, and others); (ii) mortgage (assets); (iii) personal guarantee; (iv) group collateral or social collateral; (v) third-party guarantee; and (vi) post-dated bank check. A bank can approve a loan with only one personal guarantee if it wants to, but it can also ask for more than one type of guarantee. As a loan, up to BDT2.5 million is supposed to be collateral-free, many banks ask for more than one guarantee for even small loans.

New products exist in various markets to reduce the gender gap in financial inclusion, such as gender bonds or green bonds. For example, IFC has announced an investment of up to $200 million in privately placed gender and green bonds issued by an Indonesian Bank, OCBC NISP, as part of the bank's Sustainability Bond Program in Indonesia.[76] The proceeds from the gender bond will enable the bank to increase lending to women entrepreneurs and women-owned SMEs. The green bond will support the bank to expand green financing, particularly the development of green projects and the financing of green mortgages. The bond market in Bangladesh is now evolving. NBFIs have been issuing different types of bonds, which have contributed to the growth of the bond market (footnote 18). With permission from the Department of Financial Institutions and Markets of BB, 11 bond instruments with a nominal value of BDT23.50 billion had been floated in the market up to June 2020. Developing a gender bond to support the growth of women-led enterprises would be beneficial, as this would create a fund for MSMEs that are otherwise constrained by a lack of finance.

Women SME entrepreneurs have been duly prioritized in policies, programs, and institutional arrangements (banks, training initiatives, and others). It would be appropriate and timely to similarly recognize and support other disadvantaged SME entrepreneurs. For example, BB refinancing schemes could provide special provisions to entrepreneurs with disabilities, those from ethnic minorities, and transgender entrepreneurs.

Microenterprise Development for Women and Disadvantaged Groups

All finance sector-related interventions that aim at promoting GESI should make microenterprises friendly for women, PWDs, ethnic minority groups, and transgender people. In this connection, digitally equipped microentrepreneurs should receive logistics support and training in utilizing online platforms for both product orders and payment methods. In addition, microentrepreneurs, digital service providers, distribution companies, logistics service providers, policy makers, and development partners should work together to build a countrywide supply chain connecting entrepreneurs at the grassroots level with macro franchise organizations. Such a model has already been used jointly by *Infolady Social Enterprise Limited (iSocial)* and *Manusher Jonno Foundation* under the brand name *Shujog*. The platform *Shujog* attempts to address supply- and demand-side constraints prevailing at the bottom of the pyramid or grassroots level. Such initiatives can create economic opportunities for many disadvantaged women and—if adapted to their needs and priorities—of other disadvantaged groups, both rural and urban.

---

[76]   P. Gordon. 2020. IFC Invests $200m in a Gender Bond to Empower Women-Owned SMEs. *Smart Energy International*. 27 March.

Provisions for Women and People from Disadvantaged Groups as Employees in the Finance Sector to Enhance Financial Inclusion

Human resource policies in financial institutions need to be more sensitive in terms of supporting women employees with better maternity leave and other benefits and providing various facilities that ensure safety and comfort in the work environment, to encourage them to take up and retain jobs in the financial industry sectors (footnote 58).

There should be special provisions for transgender people in the finance sector to address the demand and supply barriers to their participation as employees. Training and information programs for transgender people on financial activities will enhance their opportunities to get jobs in this sector. At the same time, awareness-raising for employers and other workers is necessary to transform the negative attitudes that disadvantage this social group.

Investments are required into developing the physical infrastructure of financial institutions specifically to increase inclusion in the sector of people from disadvantaged groups, both as workers and as users of services. This refers to a variety of types of infrastructure and facilities and includes the creation of more branches in rural areas to increase employment opportunities in this area and to reduce gender disparities in bank account holding, as well as other forms of exclusion (e.g., of rural and older people); the upgrading of physical facilities to enhance accessibility (to buildings, information, and others) for PWDs; and increasing accessibility of smartphones and internet at a low cost, for example, through the provision of low-cost loans for the purchase of a smartphone.

Strengthening Insurance Operations

Insurance products are necessary to mitigate the risks experienced by disadvantaged people engaged in SMEs, as these are the most exposed to such risks and the least able to overcome their consequences.

Special products have already been developed to meet the needs of women. For example, the Green Delta Insurance of Bangladesh offers two women-focused insurance products, in addition to general provisions. As mentioned earlier, the women-focused life insurance policy *Nibedita* offers insurance protection not only for death and accidents, but also for a trauma allowance in response to rape, bullying, and robbery. There is also a weather-based crop insurance policy to provide financial support in the case of crop loss and advice to policyholders (usually women) for production-related problems.

Such products could be adapted and developed to build economic and personal resilience among other disadvantaged groups, tailored to the specific challenges they encounter in accessing and using insurance services, and their stated needs and priorities in insurance.

Digital/Mobile Financial Inclusion

While challenges related to mobile ownership, usage, and connectivity have been identified in relation to both women and disadvantaged groups, communication technology does offer avenues to improve financial inclusion for those who remain underserved. Thus, as mentioned in earlier sections of this report, investing in digital financial inclusion could represent a means to offer access to appropriate financial services as well as to enhance access to information relevant to other aspects of the personal, social, and economic lives of groups and individuals who often suffer from marginalization and isolation. Projects to promote financial inclusion through digital/mobile technology should include the provision of low-cost smartphones or the means to acquire them, as well as training on their effective use where necessary.

Initiatives Needed to Remove the Data Gap

The discussion above repeatedly points to information gaps, especially regarding the financial inclusion of disadvantaged groups. Developing a system of recording disaggregated data on the financial inclusion of such groups could represent a start in terms of removing the barriers they face to accessing finance or using financial services. It is essential that any system developed to record the financial exclusion or inclusion of the various disadvantaged groups mentioned in this report allow for sex disaggregation of all the information, enabling an understanding of the specific challenges for women as they cut across and intersect with dimensions of age, disability, and social, sexual, or gender identity.

Conclusions

The examples and lessons presented here focus narrowly on financial services and products, and on interventions related to different aspects of the sector. Considerable attention is given to women, and especially women SME entrepreneurs, in finance policies, programs, and institutional arrangements. However, large gender gaps in the finance sector remain, and much needs to be done, from ensuring that financial inclusion activities are considered for all projects supporting women's empowerment, to matching interventions using mobile/digital interventions with the provision of smartphones and internet at a low cost. It would be appropriate to more systematically identify and support other disadvantaged groups who experience financial exclusion for this purpose also.

Some initiatives examined address both supply- and demand-side constraints prevailing at grassroots level and have the capacity to promote the economic empowerment of many women and—with the necessary adaptations—to address the financial needs and priorities of disadvantaged groups. The same applies to special insurance products that have been developed for women and that could be adapted to build the economic and personal autonomy of all members of other disadvantaged groups. In finding solutions to challenges facing women, innovations could be identified in various international best practices.[77]

---

[77] Some of these are identified at Women's World Banking.

This section of the report has also emphasized that enhancing the working conditions, rights, and benefits of women and disadvantaged groups as employees in the finance sector can enhance their financial inclusion as well as improving the overall service quality of financial institutions. Finally, it has also recommended the creation of a system of recording disaggregated data to eliminate the considerable information gap that still exists with regard to the nature, causes, and consequences of financial exclusion.

Broader interventions that go beyond finance will without doubt be needed to address more sustainably and effectively the root causes of the social and financial exclusion of women of different backgrounds and characteristics, as well as those of disadvantaged groups. A graduation approach (which originated in Bangladesh) may have the necessary scope for this task, especially when this is understood as linking together interventions on microfinance with those on livelihood promotion and on social protection,[78] and being "about upward mobility, but also and most importantly about capacity development and behavior change, without which positive graduation outcomes are likely to be short-lived" (footnote 78, p. 11). Given the focus of this report, capacity development and behavior change of all actors are here understood to refer above all to issues of GESI.

---

[78]   K. El Harizi. 2017. *Graduation Models for Rural Financial Inclusion.* Rome: International Fund for Agricultural Development.

SOME EXAMPLES OF FINANCIAL PRODUCTS FOR WOMEN

Bank or Financial Institution	Name of Scheme	Targeted Customer	Special Features
Dutch–Bangla Bank[a]	Smart Women Entrepreneurs Financing	MSMEs operated by women entrepreneurs	Low-cost loan with Bangladesh Bank refinancing opportunity, cash credit, and assisting the process
City Bank[b]	City Alo	Women entrepreneurs, salaried woman employees, homemakers, women professionals	Low-cost loan, free insurance facility, health card with discounts at clinics and hospitals across Bangladesh, personal, auto, two-wheeler loan, home loan, SME loans, Deposit Plus Scheme Account with flexible tenure
Industrial and Infrastructure Development Finance Company Limited[c]	Women Entrepreneur Loan	Women entrepreneurs under SMEs	Low-cost loan with Bangladesh Bank refinancing opportunity, dedicated desk for women entrepreneurs in SMEs
Trust Bank[d]	Ekota	Group of small entrepreneurs who are deprived of bank loan facility	Easy repayment loan; small loan for SMEs
IDLC[e]	Purnota	Women business owners	Loan facility with lower interest rate; special attention to women, facilitates women in obtaining regulatory documents and license for business, capacity and skills development of women, business management and vocational training
Eastern Banking Ltd[f]	Smart Women's Savings Account	Working women (executive, professional, businessperson) and housewives and any female Bangladeshi citizen aged 18 years or above	Modern digital banking facilities, local Visa debit card and checkbook, accident and/or life insurance coverage, discount on Mukti (SME) loan processing fee, and others.
BRAC Bank[g]	TARA Golden benefit savings account	Female senior citizens of Bangladesh (aged 50 years and above)	Easy loan, checkbook and free debit card, internet banking, SMS banking, free Insurance facility for maintaining a monthly average balance of BDT30,000, medical discount card from insurance companies to save on hospital expenses based in Singapore, India, and Thailand
	Tara TBS account	Woman banking customers	Higher interest rates on savings account of BRAC Bank, modern banking services, SMS banking, e-statement, ATM facility, cashback for grocery purchase, and others.
	Tara Business account	Women-owned business under the SME category	Card fee charged from second year of issuance date since the annual fee is fully waived in the first year for TARA customers. Hence, BDT500+15% VAT charged from the second year
			Asset or loan operations: any female sole proprietor customer will be given a TARA Business debit card by default
	Tara Personal Loan	Women of our society	Discounted interest rates, easy loan approval, credit, exclusive discount on driving lessons at BRAC Driving School

BDT = Bangladesh taka; MSMEs = micro, small, and medium-sized enterprises; SMEs = small and medium-sized enterprises; VAT = value-added tax.

Note: This table gives detailed information on various women-focused products. These are selected examples and not an exhaustive list of products.

[a] https://www.dutchbanglabank.com/sme-banking/women-enter-loan.html.

[b] https://www.cityalo.com/.

[c] https://www.iidfc.com/product-service/sme-finance.

[d] https://www.tblbd.com/retail-banking/trust-ekota.

[e] https://idlc.com/sme-loan.

[f] https://www.ebl.com.bd/retail-deposit/EBL-Smart-Womens-Savings-Account.

[g] https://www.bracbank.com/tara/.

www.ingramcontent.com/pod-product-compliance
Lightning Source LLC
Chambersburg PA
CBHW041122280326
41928CB00061B/3490